A CULTURE OF HOLINESS
FOR THE PARISH

Bill Huebsch

DEDICATION

Mark Hakomaki
A stunning experience of self-giving love

A CULTURE OF HOLINESS FOR THE PARISH
by Bill Huebsch

Edited by Mike MacDonald
Cover art © Mark Hakomaki, 2007. All rights reserved.
www.markhakomaki.com
Design and typesetting by Patricia A. Lynch, Harvest Graphics

Excerpts from the documents of the Second Vatican Council are from *Vatican Council II: The Basic Sixteen Documents,* by Austin Flannery, OP, © 1996 (Costello Publishing Company, Inc).

Scripture texts in this work are taken from *The Message: The Bible in Contemporary Language (Catholic/Ecumenical Edition),* © 2013 by Eugene Peterson. Used with permission NavPress.

© 2013 by Bill Huebsch

Published by ACTA Publications, 4848 N. Clark Street, Chicago, IL 60640. 800-397-2282. www.actapublications.com.

ISBN: 978-0-87946-519-3
Printed in the United States of America by Total Printing Systems
Year 20 19 18 17 16 15 14 13
Printing 12 11 10 9 8 7 6 5 4 3 2 First

♻ Text printed on 30% post-consumer recycled paper.

CONTENTS

INTRODUCTION

THE SPIRITUALITY OF HOLINESS DRAWN FROM THE SECOND VATICAN COUNCIL

In *The Art of Self-giving Love*, we told you about Hubert. Confronted by the slow decline and eventual death of his beloved spouse, Mary Ann, Hubert accepted his cross and entered a journey of self-giving love and dying to self that allowed him to love and care for his wife with grace. It wasn't always easy for him; Hubert was no saint. Hubert made plenty of mistakes and took many wrong turns in his journey. But in the end, he gave himself to Mary Ann selflessly. After Mary Ann finally died, Hubert felt lost and stunned, as anyone would. He had gone through an intense journey.

While he was in the midst of the caregiving and death, he was hanging on and "just getting through it." But after some months had passed and he was able to get greater perspective, a friend convinced him to make an Ignatian retreat on the Paschal Mystery. During this retreat, he looked back "over his shoulder" at all that had happened. He could then see it more clearly and he finally came to understand that embedded in that whole situation was his call to holiness. He had a conversion then, a conversion of the heart to Christ.

Hubert was an active member of his parish, but he was not a person who would have ever said he was trying to be holy. Holiness or the pursuit of such things wasn't on his horizons. He wasn't even trying to be a good Catholic. In his daily life, he marched to the beat of an inner drummer, one shaped and formed by weekly liturgy, the coming and going of the seasons of the year, and the needs of those around him. He let himself be led and he was naturally led to the practice of self-giving love, to self-emptying in taking care of Mary Ann, whom he loved dearly.

Hubert's story teaches us a great lesson. We know that we can assist people on journeys like his, to understand their daily struggles as a door opening to the sacred. People can learn to peer into their daily lives by way of a simple examination and to hear within their lives a summons to respond with love. It is, one could say, the mission of the church to assist people like this.

> Each person has received the summons to live a holy life.
>
>

The Second Vatican Council gave parish pastoral leaders (parish priests, pastors, pastoral associates, and key volunteers) this new mission. It is a mission at once simple and challenging. In chapter five of the Dogmatic Constitution on the Church, the fathers of the council forcefully remind us that each person has received this summons to live a holy life. The call to holiness is universal; everyone is called, they said.

The tone of Vatican II, in contrast to the language of the church prior to the council, leads us to interiority.[1] The council pointed the way to the inward journey. In the opening words of the Constitution on the Church in the Modern World, the council fathers wrote: "The joys and hopes, the grief and anguish of the people of our time, especially those who are poor or afflicted, are the joys and hopes, the grief and anguish of the followers of Christ as well. *Nothing that is genuinely human fails to find an echo in their hearts*" (emphasis added). Here the bishops of the council are pointing inward, asking Catholics to share in their hearts the pain of those who suffer in our world.

This also points to what they mean when they speak of holiness.

This is a remarkable departure from the pre-Vatican II church. There the focus was generally about external signs and actions. We followed rules and regulations; we kept fast days and abstained on Fridays; we ascribed to a set of theological propositions. There was always an important interior aspect to these external norms; Catholic devotional life always led us to be near to God, Mary, and the saints. But there was also the sense that, if we followed the letter of the law and believed as we were told, we would one day be with God in heaven, regardless everything else. The idea of pursuing holiness was not on our radar screens then.

We know, of course, that merely following the letter of the law is not sufficient. One can do that and still be in serious sin. For example, it is legal for a married heterosexual couple to engage in sexual intercourse. But in marriage, intercourse can be violent, manipulative, or coercive. Within marriage, it could even be rape! That it's legal does not make it loving, and the pathway to holiness is self-giving love.

At certain points, the council documents explicitly announce the added demand to go beyond the law. For example, in the Constitution on the Liturgy (article 11) they wrote this: "Pastors of souls must realize that when the liturgy is celebrated their obligation goes further than simply ensuring that the laws governing valid and lawful celebration are observed. They must also ensure that the faithful take part fully, aware of what they are doing, actively engaged in the rite and enriched by it." In other words, it's no longer enough merely to follow the letter of the law. We are called to go beyond the law into the realm of the interior life.

In chapter five (article 40) of the Constitution on the Church the bishops wrote, [Christ] "sent the holy Spirit to all to move them *interiorly* to love God with their whole heart…and to love one another as Christ loved them" (emphasis added).

In article 16 of the Constitution on the Church in the Modern World, the language is aimed even more at the interior life of the Catholic. "Deep within their consciences, men and women discover a law which they have not laid upon themselves and which they must obey. Its voice, ever calling them to love and to do what is good and to avoid evil, tells them *inwardly* at the right moment: do this, shun that. For they have in their hearts a law inscribed by God…Their conscience is people's most secret core, and their sanctuary. *There they are alone with God whose voice echoes in their depths*" (emphasis added).

But there is no more remarkable element of the council documents in this regard than chapter 5 of the Constitution on the Church. Here the bishops articulate the "universal call to holiness." Holiness, an interior journey of faith shared by all Christians, is, they tell us, what the church is all about. This isn't new. But no previous council had ever articulated it as we find it here. This isn't a mere external conformity to moral teachings or a code of conduct. Far beyond that external forum, it relates to the highest impulse of the human spirit. This council was concerned with the inward journey.

This chapter of the Constitution on the Church encountered very little resistance among the council fathers. It insists that every Christian is called to holiness and Christ himself provides the grace needed to accomplish that. Christ himself enables us to love God and love one another in a rich variety of forms. This call is *universal*. This means that the couple who is divorced and remarried without an annulment, for example, is called to be holy, and their call comes in the context of their current situation in life. It is our responsibility to help them live in daily self-giving, self-emptying love now. They belong to us and we to them because they belong to Christ. The church, or in our case here, the local parish, is much more than an enforcer of good behavior and a guardian of orthodox belief; now it must also assist everyone, *everyone*, to a life of holiness.

When we use the term "everyone" here we mean really and truly everyone. The list is long of those whom we tend to shun, ignore, condemn, or exclude in this regard. As we develop a culture of holiness within our parishes, this will be a real challenge.

Given that holiness is the work of the church, it is appropriate for us pastoral leaders to consider how we can make our parishes into "holiness centers" which both continually announce the summons and at the same time help people respond. It is not mainly a matter of instituting new programs; the programs we have now serve us well enough. Instead of thinking in terms of a program, we might simply highlight the call to holiness in everything that we already do. When we highlight it, holiness begins to pervade parish life, from homilies to teaching to outreach to the daily life of the people.

> Every aspect of parish life should help people grow in holiness in their current state of life.

We refer to this "highlight on holiness" as a process of developing a "culture of holiness" within the parish. Every aspect of parish life takes on the same aim: to help people grow in holiness in their current state of life. Now please do bear in mind that growing in holiness is an essential of the Christian life, but learning about the doctrine, moral teachings, and customs of the church is also important. This latter matter is not the subject of this short pastoral presentation. The *General Directory for Catechesis* (known as the *GDC* for short), which is our international guide on how to teach about the faith, tells us that conversion to Christ *precedes* catechesis. And once experienced, it's conversion that leads a person to undertake his or her journey of faith. A person who has not yet really met Jesus Christ and decided to follow Christ can sit in a classroom and study religion, but until there is conversion that person won't be a dedicated follower of Christ.

One of the difficulties (recognized by the *GDC*) in our present method of providing religious education, for example, is that so few of those in catechesis have experienced this conversion. As a result, their hearts are often not in the program! But even more difficult, many of the catechists we recruit also have not experienced this conversion! They agree to teach 4th grade this year, for example, but they're not in it with their whole hearts. Like the kids, they may even dread the weekly classes a little. But as article 142 of the GDC puts it: "…there cannot be teachers of the faith other than those who are convinced and faithful disciples of Christ and his Church."

"Many who present themselves for catechesis truly require genuine conversion," the *GDC* tell us in #62. "Because of this, the Church usually desires that the first stage in the catechetical process be dedicated to ensuring conversion…Only by starting with conversion…can catechesis, strictly speaking, fulfill its proper task…"

Just imagine what the church and the world would be like if we took this teaching seriously! Parish life would take on a new tone and quality, a new optimism and energy. Ministry would happen with real vigor. That, plus

The blind see,
The lame walk,

Lepers are cleansed,
The deaf hear,
The dead are raised,
The wretched of the earth
    have God's salvation hospitality extended to them
            (Luke 7:22b, The Message).

As we peer into the documents from the Second Vatican Council to construct a spirituality for the modern world, self-giving love and dying to self both jump off the page as a primary pathway to happiness and holiness.

Perhaps the most dramatic point in the outcomes of Vatican II where dying holds center stage is in article six of the Constitution on the Liturgy. Here the teaching is clear: we are *immersed* in the Paschal Mystery of Christ: we die with him, are buried with him, and rise with him. This "immersion" defines for us the meaning of baptism. When we love deeply, as Hubert did and as many of us do, we find ourselves plunged like a high diver into the waters of dying to self. Whether we can swim or not, in we go! And, like Hubert did, when we come out on the other side, we realize we have become a happy and holy person.

Let's look more closely at this. It holds the secret to our fulfillment as human beings.

In the term "Paschal Mystery" used above, the word "paschal" refers to the Passover. In that story, the Jewish people, held as slaves in Egypt, were instructed to sacrifice a lamb and mark their doorways with its blood. The blood of this lamb protected them from shedding their own blood as their houses were literally "passed over" by death. Later, in remembering this, they reenacted it by a ritual eating of lamb and celebration of an annual feast called Passover.

For the early Christians, Christ was a sign of a newly fashioned Passover, one in which we are the ones being saved by the death of Christ. In dying as he did, Christ revealed the unbelievable mercy and tenderness of God to us. His dying must be set against the backdrop of his life mission, teaching, and ministry. There we see Jesus whose mission was to set free all of us who are bound up in fear and darkness. To have embraced life as a human, he, in that very same instant, also embraced dying. Dying is part of life. You really haven't lived, one could say, until you've died.

Jesus thus revealed that God is not absent or far away, but terribly near. Hence, by his death he was not trying to win back God's lost friendship with us humans but revealing that God had never stopped loving us unconditionally in the first place. And when we use the term "unconditional," we mean truly without conditions of any kind.

Even in the darkest hour love remains with us.

God, in other words, had never abandoned or left us. Even when we did not live with love as our primary way of being together, love remained with us. Love never leaves us. Even in the darkest hour, even when hatred and meanness seems to be winning, even then, love (which is to say, God) remains with us. Life is stronger than death and love stronger than hate.

In a very real way, this is what holiness leads us humans to as well. Hubert did not stop loving his dear Mary Ann. Was he angry? Disappointed? Terribly sad? Yes, of course, he was. But the way in which he continued to love her despite her inability to return that love is a pretty strong parallel to the way that God loves us.

If you turn your heart ever so slightly toward the light, you will find God (which is to say, love) is waiting there for you. Just pause for a moment right now and let your prayer-ful glance fall on that divine love. Let it well up within your heart. Become conscious that you are connected eternally to this wellspring of love, which never ceases to be offered to you, regardless your response.

This is good news indeed, but many people in our parishes who bear daily suffering and are called on to sacrifice themselves do so without the power and comfort of this essential reality. They die to themselves alone.

The dying of Jesus is not the conclusion of a divine trans-action with the human race in which "God the Boss" demand-ed that his own son be killed in order to appease his anger. It is much more a moment of distinct and profound revelation. This is revelation that we have never seen before in human his-tory, and revelation we will never see again. It is the final word on human life, happiness, fulfillment, and all things related to salvation. We are saved, not from the Father of Jesus or his wrath but from our own selfish selves.

Have you ever done something really quite bad? Of course, we all have. Or have you ever found yourself repeating the same selfishness over and over again? Maybe it was related to sex, or about eating, drinking, spending, or lying. Maybe it was about hoarding your money even while so many suffer pov-erty. Maybe it was always putting yourself first or, even worse, not realizing that you were putting yourself first. Maybe you weren't paying attention to those around you, or were holding grudges against them, or had prejudices against those whom you judged to be morally inferior to you. Have you ever found yourself saying, "Oh, how I wish I could be freed from this. I know it won't ever make me truly happy..."?

Or maybe, as Hubert was tempted to do, you just wanted to give up on love. You decided that it was too much work, too much dying, too much to ask of anyone. Giving up on love is commonplace these days; changing diapers for our confused and belligerent spouse is not easy.

Well, as you learn to die to yourself and join your own heart to that of Christ, you will gradually find that you can indeed be freed and find the strength not to give up. Chapter 5 (especially articled 42) of the Dogmatic Constitution on the Church from Vatican II makes clear for us that the pathway to holiness is self-giving love; it is dying to yourself and letting the divine force of love become the prominent force of your life.

Thus, in Christ we are led to become paschal ourselves, led to become lambs ready to sacrifice ourselves through love.

And in the term "Paschal Mystery," the word "mystery" refers to how Jesus taught us this would all unfold. It seems like "opposite thinking." We are first if we are last.[2] We don't hate and kill our enemies, but we love them.[3] By letting go of ourselves we get our full selves in return. We find happiness by giving our wealth to the poor[4] and following in the footsteps of Jesus, himself a man who was gripped by amazing graciousness, generosity, and mercy. We don the apron and wash one another's feet[5], change one another's diapers, tend one another's needs, and remain always watchful to see more clearly what those needs are.

It is a mystery to us that being lamblike — being willing to sacrifice ourselves, being ready to go the extra mile[6] and forgive even those who harm us[7] — can lead to holiness and happiness. It is a mystery but it's a mystery of depth, not of misunderstanding or confusion. We simply cannot plumb the depths of God's love. How could anyone love this much? How could Jesus do it? How can we love that much?

How did Hubert do it? Well, to begin with, he wasn't always perfectly loving. No one is. But in the sweep of those seven years of caring for his wife, love dominated his life. His own prayerful faith was the basis. He had faith in what he could not see. He certainly didn't know where this would lead him. But, and here is a key point, the encounter with his wife was also and at the same time the encounter with Christ. Christ is found in the energy of love which we share with one another.

We must remember that the initiative to love is always on God's part. We tend to want to think that we are the ones who can save ourselves from ourselves. We think that if we just work hard enough or long enough we can overcome our own selfishness and make ourselves happy. But we believe and experience that all the initiative in this is from Christ. Christ first loved us (1 John 4:19), and the energy of love we have is only possible in Christ. Hubert knew this instinctively. The drumbeat he was following was not his own cadence. He allowed himself to "fall in line" behind the bigger force which called and guided him. He simply let go of his own dreams and plans, and willingly took on the task given to him in that mysterious unfolding of life. He died to himself.

The energy of the love we have is only possible in Christ.

This is the first principle of holiness we draw from Vatican II; the Constitution on the Liturgy in which this is found (article 6) was the first major document on which the bishops worked in the very first months of the Council. The call to holiness via self-giving love became the leitmotif[8] of every reform the Council undertook. They based their effort to renew the church on the Paschal Mystery. Bishop Ray Lucker, who was present in Rome for the Council, later said that when he realized what this meant he went through a personal conversion. He had always thought of faith as giving assent to a group of theological propositions, but after he realized the deep truth of the Paschal Mystery he began to think of faith as our response to the encounter with the living person of Jesus Christ.

The bishops at Vatican II go on in article six to say that the early followers of Christ were so centered on this mystery that they baptized those who experienced and believed in its saving power. Likewise, they shared in the Eucharist together, which was the full celebration of the sacrifice of Christ for us. It was both in their loving actions (living out the Paschal Mystery) and in their worship that they came to know their profound call to "be church."

We might say that the encounter with Christ and the Paschal Mystery are the central experiences on which our faith rests. As Bishop Lucker came to realize, this is not merely some theological proposition. It is instead what connects us here and now to the very person of Christ who lives among us and is very near to us — and therefore it also connects us to one another in love. The Paschal Mystery is not a theory of faith, but an actual practice. It's what we do: We die. We are buried. We rise. And we go out to love the world.

Later in the Council, as the bishops were working on the Constitution on the Church in the Modern World, they described the dignity of the human person, proclaiming that the mystery of humanity becomes clear only in light of the Paschal Mystery. Christ has opened up a pathway for us to follow, the bishops wrote in article 22 of this constitution. This pathway is that of dying to self, enduring the uncertainty of the grave, experiencing the joy of new life, and responding to this by loving the world. "If we follow this path, life and death are made holy and acquire a new meaning," they wrote.

This is Hubert's story. It's also the story we are all called to live.

In article 22 cited above, the bishops wrote that, "The

Christian is certainly bound…to struggle with evil…and to suffer death — but as one who has been made a partner in the Paschal Mystery and as one who has been configured to the death of Christ. The Christian will go forward, strengthened by hope, to the resurrection. All this holds true not only for Christians but also for all people of good will in whose hearts grace is active invisibly." In other words, the Paschal Mystery is not meant only for Christians, but for all people. We must all die to ourselves if we are to have human dignity. We must all love our enemies and do good to those who hate us. We must all be last, all take up our crosses, all sacrifice ourselves. There is no dignity, you might say, in lording it over others and dominating them but only in being the servant of all. Mystery, indeed!

> The Paschal Mystery is what gives meaning to life.
>
> ❧

This theme emerges throughout the Council documents and is certainly the key to a spirituality articulated through them. The church, they wrote in the Decree on Missionary Activity article 10, has been sent by Christ to reveal and communicate the love of God to all individuals and to all peoples.

In other words, not only is the Paschal Mystery central to us, but it is also what gives life meaning. Only when we love, only when we give up ourselves and die to self, can we find the meaning of life. Jesuit father and Council theologian Karl Rahner, SJ, referred to the idea that everyone is called and given the grace of self-giving love as a "universal existential." In other words, to be human is to be invited to live in the power of divine love. It is, in fact, what makes us most fully human.

As we have implemented Vatican II in the decades since the Council closed, we have tended to focus on "external matters": rubrics, structures, rites, and buildings. This spirituality of holiness, of joining ourselves to Christ in self-giving love lived on a daily basis, leads us as it did the Council to "internal matters." We want to create a culture in our parishes which supports and builds up such holiness.

CHAPTER 1

HOW TO LAUNCH AND SUSTAIN
A PARISH CULTURE OF HOLINESS

How can a parish launch and sustain a culture in which the call to holiness is sounded often and people are helped to respond? This would be a culture of self-giving love and dying to self, corporal and spiritual works of mercy, hearts dedicated to the poor, times of shared faith and prayer, fasting, and almsgiving.[9] Indeed, article 42 of the Constitution on the Church connects the self-emptying love of Christ with the very love we are also called to have for one another. Such love, the Constitution says, directs and gives meaning to all the ways we grow in holiness. "Hence the true disciples of Christ are noted both for love of God and love of their neighbor," it says.

The avenue to living with such self-emptying love, article 42 tells us, has these dimensions:

1. We must hear and know the Word of God, making it part of our everyday lives. This requires learning the art of spiritual reflection, which is something we gain through a culture of sharing faith with one another in our parish communities. When we are called on to break open the Word with others, the skill to chew on the Word and incorporate the values of the Gospel into our lives grows.

2. We must take part in the liturgy often, and for this reason, the most often repeated principle of liturgi-

cal reform articulated by the council fathers was full, conscious, and active participation by all the faithful in the liturgy of the church.[10] Regular, active participation in liturgy sets a cadence or drumbeat in our lives. Like members of a marching band, after a while we stop consciously hearing the down beat of the drummer, but we keep marching in step anyway. A parish culture of holiness provides this regular drumbeat.

3. There must be personal prayer, self-denial, and active service to others, according to article 42. These three are closely connected. Helping people grow in these three areas is the task of homilists, teachers, and leaders. Likewise, the holiness of the common people of the parish also provides a witness to the leaders. We model holiness and call one another. And we know that people grow in their ability to sustain this by taking part in a small group of some kind. Just as in Alcoholics Anonymous, where those in recovery grow by meeting together and "working the steps," so in a parish, we meet together and "work the steps" of the Christian journey of faith. A culture of holiness not only provides for this but also expects it.

It is, therefore, the true mission of each parish to be a place that focuses on holiness in many and varied ways, and teaches about it to all members. The parishioners, then, having been touched deeply with the power of conversion and self-giving love, will reach out to those in their households or neighborhoods, in their places of work, study, or recreation. They will reach out by living their own lives convincingly and speaking of their faith when appropriate. As Pope Francis has suggested, when this happens, others will be attracted to self-giving love and, little by little, their outreach will change the world.[11]

The only way we can understand Pope Francis' mission is to grasp what he means by personal conversion, and specifically in the stunning and life-changing Jesuit tradition of the change of heart. Only when we change our hearts and redirect them to self-giving love can we change the church. This is true because for Pope Francis, *we are the church*. This is the lesson of Vatican II for this pope: it wasn't about changing structures, roles, and rubrics, but about having a heart for the poor, turning our own hearts to Christ, and practicing self-giving love with Christ as our model and source of grace.

This is the pathway to holiness. Only when the church is filled with people who are living in such holiness can we change society and culture. How we pray, how we make decisions, what we believe about God, and how we live everyday life are all part of the holiness equation. Ignatian spirituality, in which Pope Francis was trained, sees God as actively involved in the world and intimately involved with us in every moment and place. And it calls us to personal conversion. It's not a mere theory of spirituality but an actual lifestyle.

> There is no way around the need for a converted heart.

For Pope Francis there is no way around the need for a converted heart. For him, the mission of the church has holiness at its center. Self-giving love costs us; we must bear our cross in order to love like that. But it also offers the promise of peace, happiness, and life after death. Pope Francis explained in *On Heaven and Earth* that holiness is essential to leadership in religious organizations, saying it is a springboard to the transcendent. "With regards to religion, holiness is unavoidable for a leader," he said.

What is a parish culture of holiness?

Hubert's parish was not able to help him experience conversion or understand his own suffering in terms of the Paschal Mystery. He'd been a member of that parish throughout his life and throughout Mary Ann's slow decline and death. He went to Mass, took part in parish devotions, and prayed in his own way at home. The parish gave him a lot: it provided regular worship, education for their children, and a place to hold family weddings and funerals. It also provided that drumbeat, that cadence, which served Hubert so well by setting a direction of faith in his life.

But he had to go outside the parish to a retreat center in order to experience personal conversion to Christ and to learn about the Paschal Mystery. Had this parish fostered a culture of holiness, Hubert could have come to terms with all this much earlier. We can't fault the parish for this. Catholic parishes in recent centuries have not generally been "holiness centers" for their people. Conversion to Christ was believed to have occurred at baptism; as long as people met all the requirements of canon law, followed the teachings of the church faithfully in matters of doctrine and morals, and gave good example by their lives, they were considered "good Catholics." What else could be needed?

But just think of all the people carrying burdens as Hubert did who are living without the benefit of this wonderful good news in their lives! Just think how making parishes into holiness centers would benefit the work of Christ in today's world!

Likewise in seminaries and schools of theology. Hubert's theologian son, Tom, had not himself experienced Christ in the profound way Hubert did on the retreat, but neither had Hubert's pastor. Most parish priests did not. Members of religious orders such as the Jesuits, Franciscans, Benedictines, and others did often come out of a greater holiness tradition because of their formation programs. But in general, even religious priests, brothers, and sisters who worked in Catholic parishes did not extend the holiness traditions of their orders to parish life.

In fact, after the retreat, when Hubert would have turned to his parish for support, there was no culture of holiness there to sustain his renewed faith. The staff of Hubert's parish was focused on organizing programs and making sure everyone got all the sacraments they needed when they needed them. But there was very little shared prayer, very little sharing of any kind, and very little focus on conversion of the heart to Christ and all that involves.

Of course, like every Catholic parish, there was a focus on the Paschal Mystery in Hubert's parish. But it was restricted to the end of the season of Lent, and there was no avenue for parishioners to travel if they sought to figure out how to incorporate this into their daily lives. It remained a largely external belief for most people.

In Hubert's parish, which was very typical, everything from the liturgy to the education programs to the business office operated in an unarticulated "culture of parish." It was a culture of efficiency: everything always got done. All the babies got baptized; Lent was always observed; and the summer festival always made its income goal. But this parish culture inadvertently also allowed people to move through life "alone together." It allowed people to attend Mass without giving their whole heart to it. It allowed young parents to get their babies baptized without really having faith themselves. Often, these young parents did not appear at the church again until First Communion time. People could live their entire lives in that parish without ever sharing their faith with another parishioner. Only the youth ministry and confirmation programs invited participants to make retreats. These youth retreats were powerful and life-changing, but when the young Catholics came back to the parish, they did not find a culture of holiness eager to support and sustain their new enthusiasm.

In other words, the culture of the parish was one that allowed its members to live and die without that encounter with Christ which leads to conversion and community.

For Catholic parishes, the strongest single force which determines what happens, who is involved, and what outcomes to expect, is usually not the budget or strategic plan. It's often not the parish mission statement; not the homilies; and not even the parish priest. It is almost always that "parish culture" we've been discussing. Parish cultures are developed over time and often without the intentional guidance of the leaders. The culture is the parish atmosphere, the set of attitudes that prevails in the parish. It's a patchwork quilt of "messages" which are sent — spoken or unspoken — to members, visitors, and even to the local community or neighborhood in which the parish is located.

> Talking about our lives through the lens of the Paschal Mystery requires that we encounter one another and, at the same time, Christ.

In Hubert's parish, the culture did not make many demands on the people. It did not make the call of Christ that we all die to ourselves a center point of its teaching. Most members of Hubert's parish could live their whole Catholic lives there without ever being challenged to share their faith and examine their lives from the point of view of how God might be calling them to self-giving love. Talking about our lives through the lens of the Paschal Mystery (which Hubert finally did on his retreat) requires that we encounter one another. But remember, the encounter with one another in this way is also and at the same time an encounter with Christ.

Sharing faith is personal and intimate; we tend to shun it a little. It's much easier to simply make sure all systems are running in the parish and that all the work gets done — and most people prefer that. Like many Catholic parishes, most members of Hubert's parish believed that faith was a private matter and that there was no need to talk about it. A sort of "culture of privacy" prevailed and was supported by a lack of focus on conversion. This culture all developed quite by accident in Hubert's parish. No one intentionally made that the goal; it simply emerged. Conversion to Christ fell off their radar screens.

It did until Hubert made that retreat. He returned with such enthusiasm to the parish that he could see with clear eyes that others in his community would also benefit from a retreat like the one he made. He knew that getting together weekly in a small group would sustain him in this excitement and faith. He knew that liturgy had to really speak to his heart now. He could not be content with lackluster Sunday Masses where people mumble the responses, only a third of the people sing, and almost everyone skips past the cup at communion time. He wanted more now. He wouldn't have called it this, but what he wanted to do was to change his parish culture.

Hubert became the evangelizer of his parish. He attended committee meetings, spoke about this to the parish team (who were mainly volunteers), and convinced a dozen of his friends in the parish to make the same weekend retreat he had made. Within a half year, he had a small and powerful group of like-minded retreat alumni, on fire with love and ready to change parish life. Behind closed doors, the parish team and pastor felt Hubert was pushing too hard. They couldn't really see how this fire of lively faith could be of help to the parish. They didn't see it, but they did see the sincerity and generosity, the self-giving love and charity of this new small group of parishioners.

After a year of prodding and pushing, the parish agreed to host a parish-based retreat for 35 people. Hubert and his crowd did the recruiting and, in the end, 37 people signed up, including the pastor and most of the team. On this one-day, twelve-hour retreat something very powerful happened. Following the format and design for the retreat in the kit they used (the *Sanctus* parish-based retreat), all present shared their own summons to love, their own need for conversion to Christ, and their own call to holiness. By the end of the day, the fire was lit! Hubert, who had spent the day helping cook and clean up in the kitchen, was thrilled. Within two weeks, the first follow-up small groups were meeting using a program called *Come to the Table*, and Hubert was in one of them.

CHAPTER 2

DEVELOPING A CULTURE OF HOLINESS

Pope Francis began calling the church to a new level of holiness within hours of assuming his role in 2013. He asked the church to be for the poor, to be more simple and less focused on pomp and ceremony. He called on everyone[12] to live with what he called "middle class holiness," meaning that we are to peer into the activities and people of our everyday lives to hear the call to holiness that echoes there.

Developing a culture of holiness within the parish leads to very specific steps or actions in the parish. These specific acts of leadership begin with the parish priest or pastor, other parish priests, and deacons; active staff of the parish (whether full-time or part-time); all the leadership folks who are on committees, councils, or commissions; catechists, teachers, youth leaders, and liturgical volunteers; members of men's or women's groups; young parents with children in faith formation; and others. A culture of holiness affects everyone. It is an orientation which the parish develops; the parish orients itself around announcing the summons to holiness, helping people peer into their daily life at home, work, and in the community to see in what ways the call to self-giving love is embedded there. This is all rooted and sustained in the sacramental life of the church.

This is a key, so let's repeat it. The parish takes on a new orientation, or a new focus, or it adds a "holiness highlight" to everything it does. It centers on the faith sharing and prayer which leads members to ongoing conversion to self-giving love, dying to self, and fidelity. And it sustains people's experiences through liturgies, small group gatherings, pastoral care, and projects to protect the vulnerable and poor.

After the change to a culture of holiness in Hubert's parish everything seemed to have more energy in it. The singing and prayer at liturgy was full-throated; parish groups raised money constantly for the poor, homeless, unmarried moms, and water projects in the third world; people truly grew to love one another and this showed. The Sunday Mass was profoundly participatory and exciting every Sunday. One Sunday morning, a visiting couple leaned over and asked one of the regulars, "How did you get your people to participate like this?"

"We introduced them to Christ," was the answer. People who are "in Christ" don't need to be told they should sing together at Mass, or pray together, or offer their money for the common good. They don't need to be asked twice to share their "daily life of holiness" in small groups. They desire all these things, just as Hubert did, because they know it leads down the only avenue to human fulfillment and happiness.

In the end, it's all about the Paschal Mystery. Any spirituality grounded in Vatican II must therefore be grounded in this Paschal Mystery. This is a life-changing, radical posture toward the world and its people, just as Jesus also faced the world with unconditional love. This frightened those who ruled the religious institutions of his day and seemed downright mad to the common people. His stories were about rescuing lost sheep,[13] including the outsider,[14] and forgiving a wayward son.[15] This is all a great mystery, indeed.

It's paschal because it calls on us to be lamblike in our willingness to give of ourselves, just as the blood of the sacrificial lamb marked the doorposts of the Hebrew people in Egypt, allowing death to pass them by. So for us, we must be lamblike ourselves: willing to "be the big one" or to "go the extra mile" or to die to ourselves out of self-giving love.

And it's a mystery because it involves "opposite thinking," which means we must be last if we wish to be first, we must forgive our enemies, we must give away our money, and we must let ourselves be salt for the earth. This is not how most cultures in today's world think; it's opposite the idea that we should always make ourselves first, always attack our enemies, and always keep our money and get as much more as possible.

Jesus' thinking is, therefore, revolutionary. As a parish we're going to end up doing things we would not otherwise consider. Our welcome mat will truly be out every single Sunday. Our money will be spent first on others and last on ourselves. Our time will be used to reach out to those who feel we do not love them. There will be a soup kitchen in our basement.

> How can we welcome all in the name of Christ when we believe others are not as worthy to be welcomed as *we* are?

I think this still frightens some church leaders today. How can we possibly welcome all in the name of Christ when we believe deep down that all are not worthy to be welcomed, or at least not as worthy as *we* are? We often prevent those most in need of grace from the very fountain of that grace which is the church and its sacraments. We draw firm lines between insiders and outsiders, lines which would be strange to Jesus. Sunday Mass is the real test for us. We hold at arm's length or just exclude people who, in seeking love, have landed outside our legal boundaries. We exclude those whom we consider to be "sinners" while we welcome the rich and comfortable. This is opposite thinking indeed, but it's opposite the thinking of Jesus.

Is this really what Jesus would want? Remember, the story

of Jesus' dying is not so much a story about God demanding the bloody sacrifice of his own son in order to be appeased and more a story about how we kill love when we see it. We must keep repeating this to ourselves. It's a story about us. And this is the shocking reality. We don't want this story to be about us. We want it to be a historical event, now done and over, which we can learn about but also from which we can keep a comfortable distance. We want to spin theological doctrines and complex soteriologies[16] around this, but we do not want it to change us.

Rather than remaining satisfied with ourselves, we must give up that security and trade it in for the absolute insecurity of the Paschal Mystery. Rather than hosting meals at which some are welcome while others are not, we must give that up and trade it in for the kind of meals Jesus ate, with all kinds of folks welcome at the table. We should recall the words of St. Augustine as adapted by Jesuit Father Karl Rahner, SJ: "Many whom God has, the church does not have. And many whom the church has, God does not have."

We can safely assure all that they are welcome with us. We could resolve the question of who's welcome to receive the Eucharist by inviting *everyone present* to come forward in the communion procession. If they are not receiving the Eucharist for any reason, they can simply place a hand over their heart and bow reverently. This is very welcoming. It's hard to be in the assembly on Sunday and just sit there when everyone else gets up for communion. This allows all present to come forward and join in the procession. And it allows folks to sort out their own consciences, as we are all called to do before receiving communion, so that even folks who might regularly receive, on a given Sunday, may choose not to.

During his general audience on May 29, 2013,[17] Pope Francis discussed this situation in the church. "The church is the great family of children of God," he said. "Certainly it has human aspects from the members who comprise it, pastors and faithful. They have defects, imperfections, sins. Even the pope has them — and he has many — but what is beautiful is that when we become aware that we are sinners we find the mercy of God. God always forgives. Don't forget this. God always forgives."

God's plan, the Pope said, is to unite all humanity into one family where everyone recognizes he or she is a beloved child of God: "The church is born from God's desire to call all people into communion with him and to participate in his divine life." We know that participation in the life of God is offered to everyone; it is a universal offer.

Noting that many people today complain about the church, Pope Francis urged Catholics to ask themselves several questions: "How much do I love the church? Do I pray for it? Do I feel part of the church family? What do I do to make the church a community where everyone feels welcomed and understood, everyone feels the mercy and love of God who renews life?"

In his morning Mass homilies in the days leading up to the audience, the pope had been speaking about the "parish culture" that Catholics should develop in order to best serve those who come to their parishes for help.

Celebrating Mass with Vatican employees that same day in the Saint Martha residence where he lives, Pope Francis spoke of the danger and the temptation for church leaders to forget that God is acting in people's lives, as his fellow Jesuit Karl Rahner, SJ, said during the council. God is acting; we are offered a pathway to holiness by God through Christ. The offer is not made by us, even those of us who work for the church.

"The triumphalism of the church stops the church," said Rahner. It becomes a church that journeys only halfway to its goal of salvation because people become satisfied with everything being "well-organized — all the offices, everything in its place, everything beautiful, efficient."

During his morning homily just a few days before this, on May 25, 2013, the Pope spoke about the importance of priests, parish workers, and parishioners creating a culture of openness and welcome for those who come to the parish asking for something.

Think of the good Christians, he said, people of good will. A young couple comes to the parish to get married. They meet the parish secretary. They are greeted and they stammer out their request: "The two of us," they say, "we're boyfriend and girlfriend and we want to get married." "Instead of saying, 'That's great!' they hear, 'Oh, well, have a seat. If you want the Mass, it costs a lot...' This, instead of receiving a good welcome." Then the Pope continued, "It is a good thing to get married! But instead they get this response: 'Do you have the certificate of baptism?'"

People often come to us in their hour of need and they find a closed door. "When this Christian and that Christian has the ability to open a door," Francis said, "thanking God for this fact of a new marriage," instead we drive them away. "We are many times controllers of faith, instead of becoming facilitators of the faith of the people," he pointed out.

"Think about a single mother who goes to church," he went on in this homily. "She goes to the parish secretary and she says: 'I want my child baptized.' And then this Christian... this Christian," Pope Francis repeated in disbelief, "says: 'No, you cannot because you're not married!' But look, this girl who had the courage to carry her pregnancy and not to return her child to the sender, what is it? A closed door! This is not zeal! It is far from the Lord! It does not open doors! And so when we are on this street, have this attitude, we do not do good to people, the people, the People of God; but Jesus instituted the seven sacraments, and with this attitude we are establishing the eighth: the sacrament of pastoral controls!"

"Jesus is indignant when he sees these things," said the Pope, because those who suffer are "his faithful people, the people that he loves so much."

Too many times, the Pope said, "we are faith-checkers instead of facilitators of the people's faith." He suggested that such a culture of parish does not sufficiently meet the demand of the universal call to holiness.

> "Too many times we are faith-checkers instead of facilitators of the people's faith."

"We think today of Jesus, who always wants us all to be closer to him, we think of the Holy People of God, a simple people, who want to get closer to Jesus and we think of so many Christians of goodwill."

Instead of opening a door, these parish people close the door of goodwill. "So we ask the Lord that all those who come to the church find the doors open, find the doors open, open to meet this love of Jesus. We ask this grace."

Blessed Pope John XXIII also seems to have captured this in his own spirituality. One day, in private conversation,[18] Pope John confided to Monsignor Guerry, the Archbishop of Cambrai, his grief that so many people of good will in the world thought that the church rejected and condemned them. Then, showing him the crucifix on his table, John said with emotion: "But I must be like Christ. I open wide my arms to embrace them. I love them and I am their father. I am always ready to welcome them." Then he turned and faced Monsignor Guerry directly. He said: "Monsignor, all that the Gospel requires of us has not yet been understood."

This opening wide of doors and arms to welcome all people is a requirement of the Gospel that, in the early 1960s and again today, many cautious leaders in the church fear will ruin all the church stands for. Pope John opened his arms wider than our human prudence would have permitted. He called all men and women "his children" and welcomed them without inquiring about their status. Pope Francis has done the same. Both popes have welcomed and loved openly. They have shifted our horizon from propriety to service. Sometimes the church itself must die to itself in order to help people cultivate holiness in their own lives.

CHAPTER 3

THE ELEMENTS OF A CULTURE OF HOLINESS IN PARISH LIFE

When there is a culture of holiness within a parish, two dynamics are always at play. First is *the call.* In every moment when this is possible — leading, preaching, teaching, reaching out, working for the poor, and others — leaders will help people hear the call to holiness which is embedded in a hundred moments of daily life. This call doesn't come (normally) from the clouds in a loud voice. It is contained within our daily life, and we must be attuned to it in order to hear it. This attuning, this formation, is what church leaders do. And again, this call is universal, meaning that it goes out to all, no matter what their situation in life.

Calling people to holiness is a skill we must all learn, and there will be more about this later in this book. The key, as we just saw, is that *God* does the calling *through us.* In the RCIA's Rite of Acceptance,[19] which is that moment at which those who wish to deepen their own conversion take an early step and formally begin their journey of faith, we pray in these words: "Father of mercy, we thank you for these your servants. You have sought and summoned them in many ways and they have turned to seek you. *You have called them today and they have answered in our presence*" (emphasis added).

In a parish which is cultivating a culture of holiness, the call goes out at every possible occasion. It would be issued, for example, when a couple presents a baby for baptism. Rather than focusing primarily on the rite itself or on who can be a sponsor, the focus would become that one which Hubert called his parish to: helping these young parents understand, experience, share, and live according to the Paschal Mystery, according to the summons to self-giving love. The focus of baptism preparation would be on conversion to Christ and how that's lived in everyday household life.

The call would also be issued to parish leaders who volunteer their time. Rather than just expecting them to "get the work done," a new focus would be placed on holiness as the real business of the parish. Just as clergy and religious make annual retreats, so would all parish leaders. Faith sharing, which is the moment at which we turn our hearts, would become common. The parish would develop into a sort of "religious community," which is really what a parish should be. Historically, religious orders often emerged because there was a great need in the church to return to holiness as its chief work. Maybe today, the new form of religious life for the modern church is actually parish life in a culture of holiness.

> We must help people respond to their call to holiness.
>
>

This call would also be voiced in each homily, each teaching or catechizing opportunity, each time people gather to staff a soup kitchen, fill holiday baskets for the poor, or put on a breakfast to raise money for the county homeless shelter. Faith sharing, breaking open the Word, and prayer would become part of each such event, along with a pause to look back over our shoulders afterward, to see how God was touching us through them.

The call is very important. It is the business of the church.

Second is *the response*. The second element at play in a parish which seeks to develop a culture of holiness is that every single person will be guided to make a response in faith. We must offer leadership and help to people so they can respond to their call to holiness. The work we do toward this end must be intentional and specific, but don't panic: it requires only a few structural changes in our current programs. It will not upset parish life and order very much. And it will not add very much to our budgets. Mainly we begin to highlight holiness in everything we do. We look at parish life with the idea that holiness is our real goal; we have the expectation that parishioners are following a journey of faith for which we want to provide road maps, rest stops, and companions.

It turns out that people who are helped to respond to this inner hunger for God, this interior urge to give themselves away in love, live together in community in profound ways. They're generous with their money; collections always go up fast in parishes doing this work. They're liturgically oriented; Sunday Mass becomes a real focal point for people. Their home lives are imbued with hospitality, forgiveness, and love. Parish life takes on a new tone and quality, a new optimism and energy. Ministry happens with real joy. Plus, as we pointed out before:

> *The blind see,*
> *The lame walk,*
> *Lepers are cleansed,*
> *The deaf hear,*
> *The dead are raised,*
> *The wretched of the earth*
> > *have God's salvation hospitality extended to them*
> > (Luke 7:22b, The Message).

Creating a culture of holiness in a parish, where the call and the response both unfold in a meaningful way, involves everyone in the parish community.

Leaders first. In treating this, we'll begin by discussing the role of the parish priest or pastor and other key leaders. We refer to this as "holiness leadership." For purposes of developing a larger culture of holiness, we consider the "team" to include the priests, of course, but also paid and unpaid ministers who work with them. This may include people who don't have a formal "job description" but who play a central or vital role in the parish.

One of the vital role leaders play in this is helping people get over the word "holiness," which many people think is about an old form of piety. When they see the leaders exhibiting authentic holiness, people are catechized by that and can begin to imagine themselves on that same journey.

Part of this will also be a consideration of "holiness homilizing" and highlighting holiness in liturgy, especially in Sunday Mass. These latter two are so vital because the Sunday Mass and homily are how the vast majority of Catholics learn about the call to holiness and how to respond with self-giving love.

The core active crowd in the parish. After that, we will consider the core leaders and volunteers of the parish, the "active crowd." These people, who now number only about 20% of registered Catholics, are really important. First, their own journey of holiness is important and we have some ways to help them on that pathway. Their journey of faith will be the basis on which we build parish life. We all know these people. We call on them often, and they respond generously. But second, these folks happen to be living with or near the 80% who are normally absent — their own family members, children, neighbors, and friends. The ones in the active crowd are the outreach workers we need to announce the good news of self-giving love and the happiness that comes from it to people who rarely darken our parish doorway. If we ever hope to invite back those who are away, or attract others who hunger for God, the active parishioners we know so well will be the agents of that.

We know them well, these active ones, but how much do we intentionally offer them retreats, spiritual direction, or even affirm the holiness of their own everyday lives, in their homes, workplaces, and communities?

The parish at large. Our third and final group will have a lot of crossover to the active group we just discussed. We want to address the parish at large, the parishioners who come for baptisms, marriages, funerals, and holidays. These are the people of good will to whom Pope Francis was referring in that May 29, 2013, talk he gave. They're doing their best to live charitably and justly, and they want formation for their children, even if they don't participate fully themselves.

This group is often composed of people whose decisions around love are out of step with church norms. They may be single parents, married to non-Catholics or non-Christians, not married at all, gay or lesbian, divorced and remarried without an annulment, or in other similar situations. Another part of this group are in good standing in the eyes of the church but their faith has grown cold. They aren't looking at life through the lens of faith most of the time. A small percentage of these folks actually do come to Mass quite often, but they come and go on weekends rather quickly (and skip a weekend here and there), and they tend to stay out of active participation in the parish beyond Mass.

It turns out that what attracts such people to vibrant faith is seeing a parish which is welcoming, energetic, and on fire with love for the vulnerable and poor. They are attracted to a parish that is authentically holy. They want to be welcomed, but not lectured about their life choices. Like all of us, they hunger for meaning, for the self-giving love that results in happiness, and need the grace to obtain it — as we all do. That grace can come to us through life in a parish which practices holiness.

Holiness practices. As we go here, we will introduce you to certain "holiness practices" which can be used within the parish in order to do the actual work of creating a culture of holiness. These holiness practices may be used in all three of the above groups. Here is a summary of them:

- † Holiness practice #1 | Leaders Sharing Faith
  The Salt of a Parish Culture of Holiness

- † Holiness practice #2 | Parish-based Retreats
  Backbone to a Parish Culture of Holiness

- † Holiness practice #3 | Regular Breaking Open the Word
  The Heartbeat of a Parish Culture of Holiness

- † Holiness practice #4 | Holiness Homilizing
  How most Catholics are introduced to holiness

- † Holiness practice #5 | Holiness Liturgy
  Making Sunday Mass a Holiness Experience
  for Everyone

- † Holiness practice #6 | Small Group Formation
  The Engine of the Parish Culture of Holiness

- † Holiness practice #7 | Mystagogia
  Seeing the Hand of God in All Things

Let us turn, first, to the leaders of the parish.

CHAPTER 4

HOLINESS LEADERSHIP

The parish priest or pastor, any other priests on the team, deacons, or the parish life coordinator if there is no resident priest, and all pastoral associates begin creating a culture of holiness by immersing *themselves* in the Paschal Mystery. Remember what the bishops said in article six of the Constitution on the Liturgy. By baptism, they wrote, we are all immersed or plunged into the Paschal Mystery of Christ. We die with him, are buried, and rise with him. The witness to faith of parish priests and staff members, and their self-giving love made visible in the parish, will lead the way for everyone else. Without such leadership, very little can happen to create a culture of holiness.

Holiness practice #1 | Leaders Sharing Faith
The Salt of a Parish Culture of Holiness

The first and most important practice that seasons the parish, almost like adding salt to soup, and prepares it for shifting to a culture of holiness has to do with the top leaders of the parish. You leaders must share your own faith often and in public. This isn't bragging or boasting; it's letting others see the faith that you have. It's "boasting in the Lord," as St. Paul put it in 2 Corinthians 10:17.

If you are a parish priest, pastor, deacon, or lay or religious pastoral associate, you may be thinking, "Don't I share my faith daily? Isn't my faith at the heart of all I do?" And the answer is a firm "yes *and* no." Yes, of course you do share your faith. You share "the faith of the church" each time you preside at or organize for the sacraments, each time you stand with a family at a turning point in life, and each time you teach about the Catholic faith. You represent and hand on the faith of the church, and thank you for doing that.

On the other side of this, however, is the other answer: no. You may find it difficult to speak about your own daily work, family, and community life in the context of your ministry: your loves and losses, your challenges and victories to practice self-giving love. This latter form of sharing faith is what we ask everyone to do as part of the journey toward holiness. But often, when it comes to the parish priest or pastor, deacon, or pastoral associate, the faith that is shared is more formal, safer, and slightly above the ordinary, everyday life we all live.

For example. Recently, I was visiting a parish where they were engaged in breaking open the Word on a parish-wide basis. (See a fuller description of this holiness practice below.) The pastor was sitting in a meeting one evening with everyone else. The Gospel reading was Luke's Beatitudes. The "question of the week" for sharing was, "When you heard the list of Beatitudes in today's Gospel, which one of them really touched your heart? Which one spoke to you most clearly?" Around the table, each shared in turn.

When it came to the pastor, he said, "Well, you all know that I'm unmarried and live alone. My brother, George, was my best friend. And you know that I'm coming up on the second anniversary of his death. Losing him was like losing my left arm in an accident: I'm not bleeding anymore; I'm healing; but I know I'll never get my arm back. I still really miss him, but today when I heard those words, 'Blessed are you who weep...' I thought, 'That's me.' But then I thought about the second line, 'for you will laugh,' and I remembered that there is hope."

Salt. Simple. It took this priest thirty seconds. He didn't preach. He'd do his preaching on the following Sunday. By becoming "one of the members of the community" for that moment, he did not diminish his priesthood but rather made himself a leader. He modeled for others what he himself believed all should do: share faith; in sharing we find ourselves converted once again to Christ. By sprinkling such sharing into parish meetings and gatherings of all kinds, this pastor "salted" parish life, creating excitement and setting the stage for a meaningful culture of holiness to develop.

Sharing faith is personal, not official.

Sharing faith is not the same as sharing theology, or speaking as an authority on the text. Sharing faith requires that we dig into our own lives and speak about what we have going on there. It's personal; it's not official.

As people continued to share around the table that night, two or three persons later, a guy whom I took to be a business person spoke up. He honestly didn't look like the "sharing type" but you never know. He said, "My brother died just a month ago in Buffalo. You really touched me when you shared, Father. I hadn't heard those words in the Gospel being addressed to me so personally, but now I see they were. Thank you."

In a parish trying to develop a culture of holiness the goal is to share the faith of the church, which we do day in and day out. But a larger goal is to reveal our own inner journey, to share from our own heart, to speak about Scripture, doctrine, or church customs from the point of view of how we experience life and faith. Instead of reporting what "we believe" you share what "you believe." It's an important distinction because when you do this, you evangelize and empower.[20]

Ray Lucker. Bishop Ray Lucker of the Diocese of New Ulm in Minnesota used to travel extensively within his diocese. Working with the pastoral center team, the diocese hosted countless forums and training days for parish leaders, all related to lifelong catechesis. In these forums, Ray sat among the people of God with the same humility, good humor, and desire for faith that everyone else had. When it was his turn to welcome everyone, he often went to the podium, opened his notes, eyed the room carefully in a moment of pregnant silence, and then spoke in words similar to these: "Good evening. I have come here tonight to tell you that I believe in Jesus Christ. When I turn my heart to Christ, I experience there a power of love, unconditional love, offered to me, and I am not a saint. I am unworthy of this love so often. And yet, it is offered continually, and I hear that offer and accept it humbly. Because of that, how could I offer you any less? How could I offer you anything other than a huge welcome and an open door in the name of Christ? I know this offer from God is grace. It is God's own very self; it is love being offered to us all. To everyone, no exceptions. So as we begin this session, let us do so by remembering Christ's love for us and our own call to practice self-giving love in return."

And then Ray would tell a story out of his own experience. "You all know I live in the pastoral center with a small group of eight others. Let me tell you, it's tough to have unconditional love for people who load the dishwasher the wrong way. But the other night as I was unloading it and, once again, dishes came out not quite clean, I said to myself, "OK. This is where unconditional love kicks in." Nonetheless, that night at supper, I did give a short lecture to everyone about the art of loading a dishwasher." Then he paused and joked, "I really need to let go of this, don't I?"

This short self-revelation, including the humor, helped everyone peek inside Ray's own life, his own daily struggles (both small and large) to live in holiness. It opened doors for people. It helped people see we aren't spinning great theologies in parish life; we aren't looking for saints. We're all on a journey of faith and, yes, it does include how we live together with people who don't know how to do the dishes.

Ray had learned how to share from his personal life. He was a natural introvert and it wasn't easy for him in the beginning, but he knew that part of his own call to holiness as bishop was to respond with *self*-giving. He knew it wasn't enough to give people an external canon of theological propositions to believe or a moral code to follow. He wanted to awaken within everyone the dawning awareness that God is giving the Divine Self to us, which happens when we give ourselves to one another.

> Bishop Lucker died to himself, opened his heart, and won the hearts of his people.

So, difficult or not, Bishop Lucker died to himself, opened his heart, and in so doing won the hearts of his people.

Parish or diocesan staff and team members (even volunteers) often get so busy with parish life they don't take part in small group formation, don't have time for much prayer, and don't see themselves as simply another pilgrim on the journey. Pope Francis has helped us see this cannot be so. In homily after homily he has stressed the need for these core, central people in the parish to define holiness as their primary aim.

Team retreat time. One strong way for core team members to keep their hearts close to Christ is to share together as a group in an annual retreat. This sort of retreat is not the same as a theological update, team-building workshop, or even a team planning meeting. The sort of retreat we propose is a true experience of deep communion with Christ, shared with one another.

Faith sharing, we have said earlier, is one key avenue to conversion. When we share our faith with others, even if we are doubtful or unsure, it somehow becomes more real for us. When we share our faith, we ourselves grow and so do those around us. This sharing, with a close friend, around a circle of companions, or in larger groups, helps us discover Christ, who is already present. Christ himself lived and worked with such companions. His own spiritual life was marked by such faith sharing.

Because we are so much in the habit of speaking mainly about what we *believe* and calling that "faith sharing," I feel compelled to point out again that when we speak of faith sharing, we do not mean sharing theological beliefs or merely the faith of the church. That is important of course, and there is a place for theological reflection. But in the story I just told about Bishop Lucker, while he did speak of his strong belief in Christ he also reached into his own daily life and told a personal story about his frustration with how people loaded a communal dishwasher! We might call this "life sharing" instead of "faith sharing," just to remind ourselves that it's in these everyday stories that we discover God is present.

Contrary to popular Western belief, Jesus was not a loner. He was not some lonely cowboy-like figure who rode around the back roads of Galilee without need of companions. Rather, he revealed God to us, the God who is love: love through intimacy, companionship, and community.

And the "community of God" which is the Trinity is the clearest revelation that we need one another. We need companions for the journey, others whose hearts we know and whose voices we trust. At the parish level, life moves fast. The schedules are packed and there isn't time for much fooling around with things that aren't in that schedule. Faith sharing is one of the things most often put off by parish staff. "There just isn't time," is the excuse.

But, of course, this excuse undermines the very purpose of the parish. Its first and foremost role is to provide a place where people can meet Christ in the life of the community. Toward that end, parishes provide Sunday Mass, catechesis, other sacramental celebrations, pastoral care, and attention to justice and peace. But it's possible to so fill parish life with activities of these kinds that Christ himself gets overlooked. It's possible to be so concerned with "getting it all done" that we fail to do the most important things: be companions with one another, share faith in Christ, grow in God's love, and allow the Spirit room to work.

Hence the need for an annual core team retreat. Let's take a look at what this retreat might look like.

Holiness practice #2 | Parish-based Retreats
Backbone to a Parish Culture of Holiness

Faith grows within us; it changes as we change. It is a gift which comes to us as we open our hearts to Christ. It abides within us, always present, as a sort of energy that lets us see light, hope, and love. In the same way spouses or partners sit together in the evening, reading or chatting, letting their love come to the surface of their daily life, so does Christ accompany us. As we experience the presence of Christ as a leading and guiding force, a desire for intimacy with Christ arises in our hearts. We find him with us in the valleys and hilltops of our lives. In the community of believers, we all have this experience and share it in common. Our faith happens in this world, not in the next. Eternity, we find, has already begun — it is *eternal* after all: without beginning or end. We aren't waiting for some sort of afterlife; we're living with faith in *this life*.

"I discovered later, and I'm still discovering right up to this moment, that it is only by living completely in this world that one learns to have faith," Dietrich Bonhoeffer once wrote.[21] "By this-worldliness I mean living unreservedly in life's duties, problems, successes, and failures. In so doing we throw ourselves completely into the arms of God, taking seriously not our own sufferings but those of God in the world. That, I think, is faith."

Retreats connect us to others on the journey and keep clear our own pathway.

Retreats help us to live our lives in this world and to do so with the power and grace of love actively guiding us. We step outside of our daily routine on a retreat, but just long enough to look back over our shoulder at it, in order to see how God is touching us. Retreats connect us to others on the journey of faith and keep clear our own pathway. It stands to reason, then, that every member of the parish core team, whether paid or volunteer, should make an annual retreat.

But it just isn't possible to send every active Catholic, every key volunteer, every team member, or everyone who wants to follow a journey toward holiness off to a retreat center outside of the parish. There isn't time, space, or money for this. Instead, we have tested resources and worked out ways for parishes to become their own mini-retreat centers. There are a variety of good parish-based retreat plans being offered today.

Examples of Parish-based Retreats. One very promising resource is a parish-based retreat process called *Sanctus*. This is a one-day, twelve-hour retreat held on the parish campus and led by parish leaders. It comes to you as an eResource which is a complete kit for putting on your own parish retreats. It's designed for people who don't know one another very well as they begin, and it follows a format we know well from Catholic tradition.

A second, related eResource kit is called *The Wheat Retreat* and it is designed for the parish team — parish priest or pastor, deacons and their wives, associate pastoral workers at every level, key volunteers, leaders, and others who already know one another quite well. *The Wheat Retreat* and *Sanctus* follow the same general format: introduction to the Paschal Mystery, small group discussions about dying to self, an understanding of how this connects to the sacramental life of the church, prayer, and learning how to make holiness a lifetime project. Both retreats close with the Eucharist.

What we like about *Sanctus* is the simplicity of it. You don't need dozens of team members, the whole parish plant, the constant attention of the parish priest or pastor, or very much money. You need two rooms, tables with chairs, and some minor equipment. The retreat kit provides everything needed for this, including supply checklists. We also like the punch it packs. People are invited to tell their "life stories" as they encounter Christ and connect that to the sacramental life of the church. It's very powerful.

Getting organized. How do you organize a parish to schedule and host enough retreats to meet the needs of the parish?

1. Schedule in advance enough retreats for everyone who needs to make one. These are one-day, twelve-hour retreats which require two rooms in the parish plant.

a. They could also be held off campus if that suited the parish best.

b. They are not complicated to host, so having one or more per month is very possible.

c. Most lay people are more available on Saturdays, so it's necessary to choose rooms that will not conflict with weddings.

d. It's also possible for people to take a personal or vacation day for the retreat, making weekdays available.

e. The closing liturgy of the retreat can also be the vigil Mass for the parish on Saturday evening.

2. You may want to follow a schedule that looks like this (in the northern hemisphere):

a. September, October, and early November: one retreat in each month.

b. December: no retreat; it's just too busy.

c. January and February up to Ash Wednesday: one retreat per month.

d. The season of Lent before Holy Week: three to four retreats during this period; it's a natural time for renewal.

e. After Easter: one or two more retreats before summer.

f. Some parishes do very well with summer retreats.

3. At the regular fall volunteer training and prep meeting, everyone is asked to sign up for a spot in one of the scheduled retreats. Make this sign-up process part of the expectation of the parish for its core leaders, including every priest, deacon, and vowed religious, as well as every layperson in parish ministry. If we are serious

about this "age of the laity," then we must raise our expectations for their spiritual formation.

The Backbone in a Culture of Holiness. As the parish leadership becomes a sort of religious community, holding and attending retreats will become part and parcel of their community life. You'll find that these retreats, being held right there in the parish plant, become a blessing to the whole parish. Within the retreat plan, a prayer coordinator calls on the entire parish to support those making the retreat. Parishioners willingly pray, make sacrifices, perform corporal and spiritual works of mercy, tend to the poor, and use sacred candles, holy water, and other sacramentals in their homes. Hence, the whole community becomes part of the new spirit of holiness. Remember, we're changing the culture of the parish to a "holiness culture," and a regular series of retreats for the core leaders becomes the backbone of that new culture.

The theme of these retreats does not change; it's always about the Paschal Mystery. In every new year of our lives we have a new experience of dying and of self-giving love to share with one another. We are challenged anew each time we share that process.

Holiness practice #3 | Regular Breaking Open the Word
The Heartbeat of a Parish Culture of Holiness

Opportunities for prayer and faith sharing at each meeting. Jesuit professor and spirituality leader, Fr. Mike Montague, SJ, used to tell his graduate students that there is a point we can identify in our human experience when the Spirit touches our hearts and leads us ever so gently toward conversion. This is a point that is available for us when we open our hearts to divine love, when we turn our inner eye to the presence of God. At that point, he said, when we say a word, whisper a secret, or share our daily experiences with one another, a miracle happens. Just at the moment we speak those words, revealing our inner selves and risking the response of the listener, our hearts turn to God and we are converted. There *in that moment* we die to ourselves, giving ourselves over to the trust of the other. We see our experience then in a new light because we see more clearly the hand of God in it.

It is for this reason that the outward sign of the sacrament of reconciliation involves speaking a word about our failure to love, confessing our sin. This is the reason we include speaking a word about our faith journey during the discussions and faith sharing on retreats. This is the reason we speak with a spiritual director, friend, spouse, or companion in order to sort out the events and people of our lives. Speaking that word is the key.

> Building opportunities to speak about our daily lives through the lens of faith is vital.
>
>

And also for this reason, building in opportunities at the parish to speak about our daily lives through the lens of faith is vital. It's why in the RCIA we break open the Word each week. We aren't attempting in that process to create biblical scholars; we're inviting people to the risk of dying, so they can experience the other side of that, the exhilaration of new life. It's a key avenue to holiness.

When we use the term "break open the Word" we mean a very specific practice. It's very close to another form of biblical prayer called *Lectio Divina*. To break open the Word, we gather in a small group and return to last week's or anticipate next week's readings from the Sunday Lectionary. We proclaim the Word within our group, and then we "break it open," meaning we see what God may be telling us through this Word for this particular day. Like the *Sanctus* retreat, the theme of Scripture never changes. We read the same readings over and over again. Each time we revisit them, we hear something new. As Pope John XXIII once put it, all the Gospel demands of us has not yet been fully understood: It unfolds week by week, year by year.

A Heartbeat of Holiness. Nothing can replace sharing faith together as a means of keeping us on the journey to holiness. Planning this for every team and leadership meeting and event creates a culture which is infectious for the whole parish. It creates a heartbeat in the parish. The leaders model this, as we said in holiness practice number one above, and the retreat process strengthens it. As each group in the parish examines each week's readings a new basis for faith is established; the Lectionary provides the opportunity for the culture of holiness to grow as, week in and week out, people are immersed in it.

Just as the retreat process is the backbone of a parish culture of holiness, drawing everyone to prayer, works of charity, and thoughtfulness about the spiritual life, breaking open the Word is the lifeblood of a parish culture of holiness, flowing through the parish, sustaining faith week in and week out. The Sunday liturgy, according to article 10 of the great Constitution on the Liturgy from Vatican II, is the source and summit of our Christian lives. From the liturgy, the Constitution says, grace is poured forth upon us as from a fountain, and our holiness in Christ…is achieved with maximum effectiveness.

Because of this, establishing breaking open the Word on a parish-wide basis is no insignificant undertaking. It is the work of the church and we should turn to it with determination.

A key component of this activity is that the people who work together as leaders and ministers in the parish become friends with one another. The love they share becomes the basis for living the Paschal Mystery throughout the parish. We should not take these friendships lightly. A parish team (paid and volunteer) is not like a group of workers in a bank. This isn't "just a job." The bonds of love and friendship shared by the team are the model for the entire parish.

As with the parish-based retreats, we know that people who invest in others and take the risk of appropriate self-disclosure about their faith and their life develop a strong sense of belonging and feel engaged with their parishes. They're very likely to remain active, to invite others to get active, and to speak about their faith when the appropriate moment arises.

How to Lead Faith Sharing. We have created a guide to help you include faith sharing based on the Sunday readings (breaking open the Word) in each meeting. Questions to stimulate this process are available on the website[22] at no charge. Over time, sharing faith on the weekly readings will create tremendous personal bonds and friendships within the group and help each one be moved by the Gospel. We refer to these starter questions as "the questions of the week."

How to Lead Faith Sharing
The Principles

1. Sunday Mass is our source. Weekly faith sharing in our Catholic parishes should flow from the Sunday liturgy — the readings, the gathering together, the experience of communion.

2. Keep it simple. When leading such faith sharing, make it easy for people to do. Do not make it into a theological discussion or speculative debate about doctrine or the Scripture.

3. Break open the Word. We are using an ancient practice of the church, as old as the church itself really. It's the method that was used on that road to Emmaus. Breaking open the Word has been restored to the church by Vatican II and subsequent renewal of the catechumenate.

4. Make the Sunday readings more available. Provide everyone in the parish with access to the readings from each Sunday liturgy. Create some starter questions to help people peer into the text and apply it to their daily lives, or use the set of starter questions provided on the website.[23]

5. Teach people how to share their faith. It is the doorway to the Sacred, the work of the Spirit in their lives, and the turning point which leads to holiness.

The Method
Breaking Open the Word Is a Two-Question Process.

The first question leads the person of faith to look into the text itself. Ask questions such as these to initiate step one of the process:

> ➢ What word or phrase struck me as I heard the reading?
> ➢ What idea or image came to mind?
> ➢ What story did I hear being told, in my own words?
> ➢ What else really touched me in this reading?

The second question leads the person of faith to look into his or her life, through the lens of the reading. For this part of the process, it helps a great deal to provide a reflection question which gets people started reading and listening to the Scriptures more intently.

This "question of the week" is very important.

> ➢ It should be a question that leads to "theological reflection" without being too theological itself.
> ➢ It should not be a "yes" or "no" question, but one that draws the user deeper into the Gospel and his or her own life.
> ➢ It should be a question that asks for a *personal* response. It's not a discussion *about* the faith but a sharing of one's *own* faith and belief. Participants should be encouraged to tell a story from their own lives.
> ➢ It should be a question that is age appropriate but still has teeth!

This two-question process is used throughout the parish for faith sharing at the beginning of each gathering:

> - when the staff gathers for its weekly meeting
> - when the finance committee gets together on Tuesday night
> - before every session of religious education during the week
> - when money counters do their work on Monday morning
> - when classes meet in school
> - when families are driving home, having supper, or finding a few moments to talk.

Thus, everyone who gathers in the parish during the week for any reason has the opportunity to share his or her faith flowing from the Sunday liturgy. Here is a four-step outline for the process.

1. The Call to Prayer
   Leader: My friends, let's pause to spend a few moments in prayer and conversation with one another. [Lead all in the Sign of the Cross.]

2. The Word of God
   Leader: May the Lord be in our hearts as we recall and re-listen to a reading from last Sunday's Liturgy of the Word. [Re-read all or part of one of the readings from the Sunday liturgy. If the readings are long, choose only a smaller part. We don't want to re-read the entire story of the Prodigal Son over and over, for example. You may also choose one of the other readings, the responsorial psalm, or one of the prayers or preface from the Mass.]

3. The Two Faith Sharing Questions
   Leader: As we consider this Sacred Scripture, I invite you to think about it in two dimensions. [You may wish to work in small groups if your number is large.]

   - First, ask about the text itself, to draw attention to the Scripture.
   - What word or phrase in this text caught your ear?
   - What story did you hear, or what image did you get?
   - What touched you as you heard this reading?
   - Second, when the first sharing is complete, ask about the people's lives. [Here you can offer a "Question of the Week" to help people get started sharing their faith.]

4. The Prayer. At the end of the sharing period, invite folks to pray in one of the following ways:

   - The Lord's Prayer out loud together
   - Spontaneous prayers
   - A moment of silent prayer
   - A recorded hymn.

Blue paper. Note that this prayer form is available on the website as a downloadable free[24] item allowing you to fill in the blanks for each week and reproduce it for everyone in the parish. Many parishes use blue paper for this weekly prayer sheet. It helps people set it apart from other printed resources. People know that no meeting or gathering will start without "the blue sheet."

Catholic Faith, Life, & Creed. There is an alternate resource for weekly breaking open the Word sessions; it's part of *Catholic Faith, Life, & Creed*. For each week of each Lectionary cycle, author Mary Birmingham provides a commentary on the readings along with a group of questions to use to break open that reading. (A free guide[25] is provided on the website to click and open.) Homilists and teachers make wide use of the worksheets in this series because of the fine commentary on each week's readings which Mary provides.

In closing our commentary on this particular holiness practice, let me re-emphasize the importance of letting the Sunday liturgy of the Word be our primary source for faith sharing and faith formation. It is the hope of the church that the Lectionary can be a fountain, flowing over into the everyday lives of the faithful, filling them with the hope and wonder of God's Word.

Holiness practice #4 | Holiness Homilizing
How Most Catholics are Introduced to Holiness

And this brings us to a related dimension of a parish culture of holiness: the homily at Sunday Mass. We want to sound the call to holiness every time we reflect on the readings. The summons we receive to self-giving love is embedded in the Scriptures and our own daily lives. When we bring these two together in a homily, we have a strong chance to help people see how pervasive and powerful that call is. As people begin to see with eyes of faith, their conversion deepens.

Pope Francis. On the feast of Corpus Christi in 2013, Pope Francis gave a homily in which he did this very clearly. The reading, if you recall, is from Luke 9:11b-17 where Jesus is host of a huge gathering (rather than the guest, which he often was in Luke) and to which everyone seemed invited. There were more than five thousand people present! The Holy Father said that there is a line in this gospel story that always strikes him. It is in Luke 9:13 and it's this one, "You give them something to eat."

First of all, he asked in the homily, "Who are those to be fed?" He said that the answer to this can be found throughout the Gospel: the crowds, the multitude, or in a word, everyone. "Jesus is in the midst of people," Pope Francis said, "he welcomes them, speaks to them, cures them, he shows them the mercy of God; from among them he chooses twelve apostles to be with him and immerse themselves, like him, in the concrete situations of the world." People did indeed follow Jesus, he said. And why? It was because he spoke and acted in a new way: with sincerity and authenticity. He was genuine. He lived what he preached and people knew it so they followed him. They were attracted to him like metal to a magnet. He gave the people hope and love.

> People followed Jesus because he spoke and acted in a new way: with sincerity and authenticity.

"Tonight," he went on, "we are the crowd in the Gospel, we seek to follow Jesus to listen to him, to enter into communion with him in the Eucharist, to accompany him so that he may accompany us." Then he asked the 'holiness question': "Let us ask ourselves: How do I follow Jesus?" The Holy Father went on to help everyone unpack this key question about holiness. He said that Jesus calls us out of ourselves and into self-giving love. We do not make our life our own, he said, but we make it a gift to others. Jesus speaks in silence in the mystery of the

Eucharist and each time reminds us that following him means coming out of ourselves and making our life not our own but a gift to him and to others.

And this is where that line came into focus for the Pope. When we see the needs and suffering of others, as Jesus did the hungry crowd, we tend to acknowledge it by saying something like "May God help you" or "Good luck with that." But Jesus calls us to a deeper level of dying to self. "You give them something to eat," he tells them.

Watch what we do. Holiness is not constituted by what we profess on our lips but by what our profession leads us to do. We may not think we can do what we know we are called to do, but in fact we do have that strength. We can do what the Holy Father called us to as he closed his homily on Corpus Christi: "Do I let the Lord who gives himself to me, guide me to come out more and more from behind my little fence, to go out and not be afraid to give, to share, to love him and others?"

Pope Francis' homily is a good example of one in which we are called to holiness, not merely to understanding a text or applying it to others. We call this "holiness preaching" and it transforms parishes.

For the one preparing the homily there are two dimensions to this. First, simply add a "holiness highlight" to your process. Always ask yourself, 'How is the call to holiness embedded in this reading, or in our society this week, or in my own life today?' Let that guide your homily preparation. Second, share from your own heart and experience. When you tell your own story to your people, the lights will come on and people will see anew what faith means. You have the chance in your preaching to shift their horizons away from believing in a distant, absent God. You can help them believe in love. When people start believing in self-giving love, in dying to self, in being immersed in the Paschal Mystery, holiness follows.

In order for a homilist or teacher to speak of Scripture with an ear to how each text calls us to holiness requires an intentional effort[26] on their part to prepare with this in mind. This does not add a great deal of effort or time to the preparation process, but it does produce a homily which supports the shift to a holiness culture within the parish.

For example. It was the 5th Sunday of Easter in Year C. It was early June and the church on that Sunday morning was crowded as usual. Babies crying, people coming and going, the late-comers crowding into the back pews. The presider was also giving the homily and it all started out as usual: a little commentary on the readings and a review of the Gospel which was from John 13, where Jesus speaks of the new commandment. "Just as I have loved you," Jesus is reported to have said, "you also should love one another." Such love would be the hallmark of the Christian and the way in which others would know that we believe in Christ.

But then the homilist seemed to put aside his notes, and he told a simple story. He told us that during the week he had been called at night to attend to a child who was very sick. The family had called for him at the hospital. As he got dressed and prepared to go downtown, he decided to call Marie, a member of the pastoral team who knew this family well and had been walking with them through the cancer of this child. He felt she would want to know. She immediately asked to ride along, and the two of them set out in the middle of the night on this errand of mercy. A hush had fallen over the congregation as they listened intently to this story.

When they arrived, the child, Alicia, had just died; the sadness was overwhelming. "As I faced this," he said in his homily, "I felt powerless and speechless. I was numb. I mean, I know I'm the priest and should always be strong, but it all brought back memories of my own little brother who died from an accident when I was just ten."

"Marie could see that I was struggling," he told us, "so she stepped forward and put herself in my place. Her love for the family, for me, and for the child was so evident. Her words made that love obvious and love took over the moment. 'The love you all have for one another,' she told them, 'never dies. It remains forever. We're all very sad right now, but we can hang on to the certainty of all this love. When Alicia died, the love she had for you and you for her — it did not die with her. It's still here, still with you, and nothing can take it away, not even death.' She was speaking to me as much as to that family, huddled in sadness and pain."

"As I was preparing for this morning's Masses," the priest continued, "Marie's words and love came back to me. Remember that this Gospel reading is told in the same chapter as the washing of the feet, when Jesus showed the depth of his love. Just listen to these words of Jesus one more time as you think of Marie: 'By this everyone will know that you are my disciples, if you have love for one another.'"

This was a "holiness homily" which left the people in the pews with a rich treasure. The priest showed us the avenue to holiness: his own humility, the story of that family, the power of love, and the self-giving action of Marie as she sensed that her pastor was himself paralyzed by this death. All of this was much more important for the hearers of the Word that Sunday than any amount of formal, critical commentary on the text would have been.

Holiness practice #5 | Holiness Liturgy
Making Sunday Mass a Holiness Experience
for Everyone

We've all experienced Sunday liturgy where the level of participation is so low we can hear only our own voice when we sing or respond aloud. We know the people present are indeed praying this Mass, but there isn't much of a community experience going on. At communion time, everyone shuffles up, but the energy remains low. Have you experienced this?

In parishes developing a culture of holiness, planning for high levels of participation at Sunday Mass is vital. We know that participation levels rise as people experience deeper intimacy and communion with Christ and one another using the holiness practices we have already discussed. Beyond the homily, the liturgy itself can include an invitation to all to bring their hearts into the prayer, especially the Eucharistic Prayer. Thinking through the liturgy from top to bottom to ask how it leads people to holiness has rich benefits.

At the door. Remember that many people do not come to Mass every week. While we certainly don't condone this, we also want to be careful to warmly welcome everyone when they do come. Many people also come to Mass with family members who are not Catholic. Again, a warm welcome is important. And there is a large group of people who may not feel very welcome at Mass on any day: because of a marriage irregularity, or because of some sense of shame they may carry, or because they have made life choices that do not reflect Catholic teaching perfectly. How can we welcome all[27] in Christ's name?

Gestures. Build in gestures during the liturgy which help people to feel as though this is their liturgy, too. Such gestures should be carefully designed so they are not embarrassing for people to do. They can be kept simple but still carry a profound message. For example, whenever the priest addresses the people during the Mass, he gestures by opening his arms. Teach your people to make a similar gesture toward him in return. As people gesture toward the presider, their own spoken response is more genuine and less "muttered." The gesture itself teaches everyone that we are "in dialogue" with the presider at this point.

Prayers of the Faithful. In one parish, the people of the community were invited to request prayers as they entered the church. Was someone in their family ill? Traveling? In any kind of special need? An editor was parked near the church entrance and took all these notes and prepared the prayers which would then be read aloud just moments later during Mass. Very powerful. For another example, could you use technology to efficiently welcome submission of prayers? And even if this is not possible, the prayers written for the faithful should reflect what's happening in the world, in the neighborhood, and in our homes. Finally, not a Sunday should pass without us praying for our neighboring Christian churches, and for all the people of God around the world.

The Offertory. How we pray shapes what we believe and how we behave. Allow everyone in the church who has a gift to bring it forward from their pew in a messy "procession of gifts." This simple gesture allows people to "own" the gifts they bring forward. At one parish, a large basket is placed on a table as folks enter the church. A sign in front of it invites people to place their offertory gift in it. The basket is brought forward at The Preparation of the Gifts. No collection is necessary. It really helps focus the congregation on the liturgical action.

A personal offering, shared. In some parishes, just as he is ready to pray the Offertory prayers, the presider invites everyone to mentally place on the altar with him any special intention they may have in their hearts that day. Then he invites them to pray with him in both thanksgiving and need.

Gracious hosts. In some parishes, the presiders and communion ministers receive only after they have served everyone else. In this way, they demonstrate good hospitality and help everyone see that they are servants of all. The response of the people to this simple symbolic act is overwhelming. As they see their ministers acting as servants, they are catechized each Sunday.

CHAPTER 5

HOLINESS FOR THE CORE, ACTIVE MEMBERS OF THE PARISH

Parish volunteers have become very significant players in the life of today's church. In the United States, parishes often employ lay or religious ministry staff people. But in most parts of the world there is only the parish priest, possibly only a parochial vicar, and all the rest of the team members are volunteers. The baptized, we believe, share in the one priesthood of Christ through what we call "the common priesthood." Distinguished from the "ministerial priesthood" of the ordained, this common priesthood is charged with much of the work of today's church.[28]

Please note here: I did not say that the members of the common priesthood are charged with much of the work of today's *parish*, although that is also often the case. It is the work of *the church*: the mission of Christ in the world, the building of the Reign of God. Forgiveness, generosity, love for the earth itself, care for the poor, and shared meals — this is the work of all the members of the common priesthood.

Do we treat this common priesthood too lightly? For so long, the ordained priest was seen as the only minister in the community. Vatican II brought forth a new focus, however, reminding everyone that baptism is the essential sacrament of ministry. The ordained priests have the role of supporting and assisting the baptized to do their work.[29] Pope John Paul II was a champion of all this. "The ministries which exist and are at work at this time in the church are all, even in their variety of forms, a participation in Jesus Christ's own ministry as the Good Shepherd who lays down his life for the sheep, the humble servant who gives himself without reserve for the salvation of all," he wrote[30] in 1988. Can you see in this statement that the Holy Father was connecting self-giving love and lay ministry? Lay volunteers share in the priesthood of Christ himself; they share in his Paschal Mystery.

When we look at all these marvelous and generous baptized members of the common priesthood through the lens of the call to holiness, it seems clear that their very ministry itself is part of their response to that summons. Think of them as a vast and multi-talented parish staff. They are that; they're also the staff people of the Kingdom of God. As such, a parish which is cultivating a culture of holiness will certainly want to help these "workers in vineyard" grow to greater holiness, too.

Toward that end, let us reflect on and summarize what we have said so far without repeating it:

1. The core, active group of parishioners will benefit greatly from the witness of the leaders, as we said in discussing holiness practice #1 above: *Leaders Sharing Faith*. These core people have a lot of contact with parish leaders. If the leaders are cynical, negative, or apathetic about sharing faith, then the core people will be, too. But if the leaders are sincere and authentic, taking appropriate personal risk and letting others see inside their journey of faith, then the culture of holiness will take off.

2. The core group will benefit greatly from having access each year to a parish-based retreat: for all the reasons we cited in treating holiness practice #2 above, *Parish-based Retreats*. The volunteers and leaders of the parish are a vital part of that new form of "religious community" we described. As such, sharing annual retreats to-

gether as part of their overall formation in faith — and allowing the wider parish to support that with prayer, sacrifices, and works of mercy — this gives real backbone to the parish culture of holiness. The members of the core community in the parish will be the leaders of these retreats for others! How exciting!

3. Likewise, it goes without saying that this core group of active parishioners will get "into the heartbeat of a culture of holiness" within the parish each time they share faith and peer into the Sunday Scriptures, as we discussed in holiness practice #3 above: *Breaking Open the Word*. Many parishes do this already and find that it does not take very long for everyone to get used to the idea that breaking open the Word is part and parcel of parish life.

4. As a core, active person who loves Christ and the church, sitting in the pew each week is vital. This is how the cadence of one's faith-life is set, that drumbeat, week after week. Central in this, of course, is the homily as part of the Liturgy of the Word, as we said in holiness practice #4 above, *Holiness Homilizing*. These active members of the parish may hear fifty out of fifty-two homilies in a given year. The effect of being called in each one to greater holiness is profound.

5. And finally, on a par with the Liturgy of the Word is the celebration of the Eucharist, the Mass. The welcome, music, community prayer, and communion itself must be designed carefully for the parish so that people can "come to it with proper dispositions, that their minds be attuned to their voices, and that they…take part,

fully aware of what they are doing, actively engaged in the rite, and enriched by it."[31] We described this above in holiness practice #5 above: *Holiness Liturgy*.

Let's turn to another holiness practice which helps build and sustain the culture of holiness within all the active members of the parish: small group formation.

Holiness practice #6 | Small Group Formation
The Engine of the Parish Culture of Holiness

Just too large. Today's modern parish is the size of an entire "diocese"[32] in the early centuries of the church. In the early years, all of Christian life was lived in what was essentially a "small Christian community." Christians by and large knew the names of the others with whom they worshipped. There was a level of accountability and transparency which made the Christian life dynamic, for the most part. But today our parishes have thousands of members, and most people worship next to folks whose names they don't even know. People in Catholic parishes often don't even introduce themselves to the people around them at Mass. The result is that many Catholics attend Mass on Sunday "alone together with others who are also alone."

Small groups to the rescue! Small groups come in many shapes and sizes. Your parish is likely already filled with them. Some small groups are formed as intentional small church communities: people who have met together for many years and formed deep bonds. Other small groups emerge from all this work we're doing on the universal call to holiness. Still others gather weekly to break open the Word based on the Sunday readings. Some are simply a collection of folks who partner together in ministry:

- The music ministers who spend time rehearsing and planning become connected to one another and form bonds over the years;

- The bereavement team whose members help one another bear sadness for others often become quite close in their ministry;

- Volunteers working on the social action committee, standing on the front lines of the fight for justice and food for the hungry, often share deeply and connect as a community.

A parish may have a retreat process in which participants share a period of formation together and then hope to continue to grow in holiness, gathering as a small group afterward. The pastoral staff and other leadership groups may include faith sharing as part of the regular meetings; that core team is the small group at the center of the other small groups.

And beyond this are people living their daily lives outside of parish activity. You could consider parents and their children, along with the family and friends who are part of their lives, to be a small group. There are many small dinner parties, people who invite one another back and forth to supper and become friends and companions in the process. There are neighborhood small groups who throw together potluck-style suppers from time to time. My family belongs to one of these and it's really important to us as a household. We started in the week we moved in by going up and down the block, knocking on doors, and introducing ourselves. We invited all the neighbors to a potluck the next Sunday night — and they all showed up! Within a week we had been invited back and met a couple living in the next block. So it goes. Sometimes the small group is workmates, schoolmates, or others. All of these less-formal small groups have a great impact on people's lives.

There are many benefits of participation in a small group, for the individual members and for the parish. Members of small groups say they join because they seek deeper faith and a stronger connection to the larger parish community. Group participants find church becomes a more essential part of their lives, rather than something that remains on the fringes of life. Members attend Sunday Mass more regularly, consider church teaching when making moral decisions, and grow more comfortable praying aloud and leading others in prayer.[33]

One time several years ago, I joined a small group to which I belonged for more than ten years. We met every Wednesday morning at 10 AM for tea or coffee, and we met for exactly one hour. We were punctual. Leaders rotated. And the program or conversation guide we followed did not change. Some members came and went from week to week, but there were generally about ten of us present on any given Wednesday. This small group saved my life. It was the stable force that sustained me through a difficult professional period. This was not a group organized by my parish; it was an Al Anon group (for friends and family of people struggling with addictions).

No matter how or where the small group forms, the key is that in our journey toward holiness, being accountable and transparent with a small, trusted group of fellow travelers is essential. The way to the heart of the Lord is seldom traveled alone.

Principles. There are some well-learned principles to follow when trying to start or sustain small groups in the parish. First, if you're the parish priest or pastor, or one of the staff members, or even an active volunteer, you should be the first one to be in a small group. Your example is what will make or break this movement in the parish. Be public about this and about the benefits to you.

Second, small groups don't have to meet more often than suits their members. Modern life is busy, and if we demand too much in this regard we will fail. I know one group that meets for supper about once a month. They gather, talk about their lives, open a bottle of wine, share a simple meal, and end when they're tired. A pastor told me recently that he meets weekly with a group of eight parishioners to break open the Word together and prepare him to preach the following Sunday. Meeting any less than weekly for this group would be too infrequent. Another group I know was formed out of the daily Mass crowd and has coffee or tea and rolls together every other Thursday morning. They use *Come to the Table* and they even meet when there is no morning Mass on a given Thursday!

> **Be public about the benefits of small groups to you.**
>
>

Third, keep these meetings simple. Affirm everything that appears to be a workable small group, even if it's the parents of kids in softball or dance class. If you use a resource aside from Scripture to provide "content" for the small group, keep that content simple. Do not buy expensive books; you don't need them and most people don't read them. We have learned that handouts work much better than books do. People don't feel overwhelmed by them; they feel they can write on a handout; they take handouts home and revisit them later; and handouts cost very little to reproduce. *Simple really works* in small group formation.

For Hubert, the small group he joined after his retreat became a strong force which sustained him. They met every couple of weeks, usually on Sunday evening, and almost always with a glass of wine or soda and shared snacks. The pastoral leader in his parish who organized this group was careful not to refer to it as a "grief group" because she knew that, for some people, this wasn't really its purpose. What Hubert shared with the group did connect, of course, to losing Mary Ann, but it was much larger than that.

This pastoral worker was clever; she didn't put together a big new program of small groups, but she gradually linked people to one another, handed them a resource, and stepped back to watch. She only intervened if there was a need. She told me that her insight for this came from her own religious community. Many years ago, her community leaders asked the sisters to gather in small groups, only coming together at the motherhouse once or twice a year. Her small group met only once a month, but it was just enough. It did not replace her need for friends or her daily prayer; it provided an anchor in her busy life and often that anchor called her back to friendship and prayerfulness.

Holiness practice #7 | Mystagogia
Seeing the Hand of God in All Things

I arrived at a parish one Saturday late afternoon to lead a 3-day parish retreat; I was there on Saturday because I was being introduced at the weekend Masses. As I was waiting in the lobby of the office, a group of folks came traipsing through who'd just returned from staffing a local soup kitchen and clothing store for the poor. Their leader was about to do *mystagogia,* a form of "spiritual evaluation" with them. I just watched. They all sat around in a circle and the leader slowly walked them back through all the steps of that day — their gathering, the drive over, the unpacking of the food, the work with the used clothing depot, the arrival of the guests, the meal, the clean-up, and the drive home. Then she eyed them in a moment of perfect silence and asked, "Who did you meet today? Whose hands did you touch? Who whispered something into your ear? What still hangs around inside you now from this day?" and other questions like that. The workers began to speak and the stories they told were downright amazing. If they had all just gone home, taken a shower, and turned on the TV, they would have missed the burning bush that was right in front of them. By pausing for mystagogia, they looked over their shoulder, as it were, at the day and consolidated the gifts they had received. This is a key aspect of the journey to holiness.

Mystagogia can be built into every dimension of parish life.

Wider use of this sort of "looking over our shoulder at the mysteries of life" is needed on the journey to holiness. We call this by the formal name of *mystagogia*, a Greek term which means, literally, *going deeper into the mysteries*. In practice, what you do is to sit folks down after an experience of some kind and ask the question, "What touched you in this?" "What did you hear and see?" Or even, "How did you experience the hand of God in that moment?"

Mystagogia or looking back over one's shoulder can be built in to every dimension of parish life. The cost is free and the outcome is dramatic as people connect the dots and begin to hear the call to holiness contained within their many experiences. Simply pause often to ask this question: what happened in your life in the last couple of days and, when you pause to look back over it, how do you see the hand of God in it? Or after a prayer or liturgical experience, ask: what touched your heart in these moments? When you look back to this liturgy, how can you recognize the ways in which God was speaking to you?

The Examen. I know a couple who has built this process into their own daily lives. Once or twice a day, they pause and review the events that have just unfolded, even if they seem quite simple. They do this without a lot of formal prayer, but they are well aware that they are in the presence of God. They simply revisit, for example, a supper they just shared with friends. They talk about who was there, about the food, and about the whole evening. Isn't this a natural thing that everyone does? But they take it one step further and often ask questions like, "What was the high point of that for you?" or "What touched your heart tonight?" This pausing to revisit the events of the day has helped them grow to see how God is present in all the people and events around them. They can also more easily hear the call to holiness embedded in all that.

The daily *Examen* which this couple learned to use is a technique of prayerful reflection on the events of the day in order to detect God's presence and discern his direction for us. The Examen is an ancient practice in the Church that can help us see God's hand at work in our whole experience. St. Ignatius thought that the Examen was a gift that came directly from God, and that God wanted it to be shared as widely as possible. One of the few rules of prayer that Ignatius made for the Jesuit order was the requirement that everyone practice the Examen twice daily — at noon and at the end of the day. It's a habit that Jesuits, and many other Christians, practice to this day.[34]

CHAPTER 6

HOLINESS FOR THE PARISH AT LARGE

We've already mentioned the importance of the core team being committed to holiness and living by the Paschal Mystery. The parish at large can see this and will be influenced by it. As the leaders share their faith, and the core group of active parishioners takes up faith sharing, a new culture emerges and members of the parish at large will be swept up in it.

One parish that came to us for a coaching about all this described their efforts to reach out to the "unchurched" in their parish.[35] We asked what they hoped to offer them. "We want them back in the pews," came the answer. I felt I could detect in this that one big reason they wanted them back was to increase the offertory collection. But as we examined life in that parish, we could plainly see that the team and core leaders really themselves were mainly caught up in an "administrative culture of parish" that had a focus on budgets, plans, programs, and income streams. Of course, there was also liturgy and education, but there honestly wasn't that much of an authentic spirit of holiness there to attract anyone back.

They were starting on the wrong end. We all want to see those who are absent and unengaged return to Sunday Mass, but we have to start that process with *us*. We have to become a magnet: a parish so authentically holy and attractive that people want to be with us. This parish asked what we thought the first step should be. We advised them to plan a *Wheat Retreat* for the priests, team members, and key volunteers, about 35 people in all. They did this; they started with their own renewal, which must occur in all seasons.

While we urged them to make this retreat themselves, we also urged them to make these one-day, twelve-hour retreats widely available within the parish for everyone who wanted them.

One of the chief outcomes of parish-based retreats is the sense of belonging it gives participants. Even a parishioner who is unknown by most in the parish, or who is new to the parish, or even one who is making his or her way back to parish life after an absence experiences a strong sense of belonging to God, to the parish, and especially to the others on the retreat. And such a sense of belonging keeps people engaged. It causes them to invite others to share the experience they had. And it creates tremendous loyalty to the parish and its needs.

Again, the regular occurrence of these easy-to-do, one-day, twelve-hour *Sanctus* retreats (plus the annual retreat for the team: *The Wheat Retreat*) forms the backbone of a parish culture of holiness.

Other retreats for youth, confirmation and RCIA candidates, parents whose children are celebrating sacraments for the first time, and others can also be scheduled. The *Sanctus* retreat is excellent for these other groups, but we recommend people attend together and not be in the general mix of parishioners. Any group with a special and unique goal such as these have will do best if they go through the process as a body.

The second step was for those leaders to begin speaking of faith clearly and publicly. We urged them to talk less about administrative details: policies, guidelines, money, and all that sort of thing. Speak less of that and be more ready to share faith. We helped the parish leaders work somewhat in the style of Bishop Ray Lucker, sharing beliefs but also telling stories out of their daily lives. This was all unfolding for this parish while at the same time the homilies were raising the profile of the call to holiness (which is to say the art of self-giving love) that is embedded in the people and events from our daily lives and announced as the good news in Sacred Scripture. These homilies were also a key feature of the new culture of holiness because they were heard not only by active parishioners but also by visitors and the folks who were only present for Mass occasionally.

We also discussed why a truly participatory liturgy is so vital. Back to that cadence: The reason we have always been so insistent about Mass attendance is no longer because rules are broken when people miss but that we all need the regular drumbeat of the liturgy in our lives, week in and week out, to guide our feet on the journey to holiness; this is the grace of liturgy. We urged them to take some brave steps to help people participate more fully.

Six months later. Within six months things had begun to change in this parish. The parish priest (the pastor) reported that his own faith had taken on a new lightness and energy. He was living more simply; he was more attentive to the presence of God in everything throughout the day; he was speaking in public about his own faith and life story for the first time in his priesthood, and people were responding with affection and love; he was seeing the role of the leader now more as "first disciple" than "the one in charge." His authority came from his authenticity, as Pope Francis has taught it would.

The most exciting shift for this parish came, however, in the key leaders and staff. They, too, were growing in their own personal faith. The retreat they had shared together had profound results in their own lives which prepared them to see what Hubert had seen: that others also longed for the encounter with Christ. They no longer looked at the absent and unengaged as "bad people who don't come to Mass" and began to see that many of them were indeed living truly holy lives and practicing heroic acts of self-giving love. They could also see how much these folks might benefit from seeing, as Hubert did, the meaning behind all this, the call to self-giving love (that is, the call to holiness) embedded in them.

The parish now had events and opportunities to invite people to become part of: retreat days, small groups, a participatory and welcoming liturgy. They had also begun to affirm people's daily lives, the place where most people live out their call to holiness. All those people committed to sports for their kids were no longer seen as the enemy, and even the sport itself was seen as a time to "coach" parents how to be "holy" with their children.[36] As the parish looked forward to its second year of planning for a culture of holiness, they had their eye on baptism preparation, knowing that many who come for baptism are not trained to hear the call to holiness in their own lives. In this, they were also talking about how to welcome a non-Catholic parent.

> Many were practicing heroic acts of self-giving love.

Likewise, they were doing serious planning for those young parents after baptism, right up through all the first sacraments. They were preparing to coach them to form their own children in faith and holiness.[37]

Next on the radar screen for this parish were the many generous catechists and teachers who came forward every year. To these they offered the usual preparation needed for the year — calendars, schedules, support materials, and so forth — but also a *Sanctus* retreat. They offered everyone a chance to choose one of three dates for this, and all but two signed up. This retreat, more than the scheduling details, prepared them for a year of "holiness teaching." By "holiness teaching" we mean that the catechists (for children, youth, adults, and RCIA) learned the skills needed to help learners hear the call to holiness embedded in daily life and revealed through church teaching.

The youth ministry and confirmation leaders were way ahead of this game in the parish! Building on decades of retreat and renewal work, these folks moved forward with real gusto. They were mainly relieved that the young people who encountered Christ on the retreats and days of reflection which they offered would now return to a parish in which the parish priest (the pastor), the staff, the core team, and the Sunday liturgy would all connect and reflect the same enthusiasm for faith they had.

The RCIA leaders were thrilled. For years and years they had been hearing at diocesan workshops that conversion had to precede catechesis, and that breaking open the Word and other such practices were essential for the RCIA and also for the whole parish. Their dreams had come true! They found themselves working in an environment now where they could truly say to the candidates and catechumens that the entire parish shared their journey of faith. The newcomers could sense it at Sunday Mass and in parish life overall.

One big element of this which was so attractive to the other Christians who were coming into full communion with them was the newly available small group experience using simple resources that led everyone to share faith.

Is there more work for this parish to do? They would tell you that they have only just begun. They can see the potential now for this renewal to deepen and broaden within the community. Many of the absent friends and family members of the parish are still absent, but word is getting out that something new and exciting is happening at St. Margaret's. The new culture of holiness is taking shape.

Hubert could not have been more thrilled!

ENDNOTES

1. O'Malley, John. *What Happened at Vatican II* (Cambridge, MA: The Belknap Press of Harvard University, 1968), pages 50-51. This is an excellent telling of the story of the Council.

2. Matthew 16:20

3. Matthew 5:43-44

4. Matthew 19:16-26

5. John 13:1-11

6. Matthew 5:41

7. Matthew 6:14-15

8. A leitmotif is a musical term referring to a short, constantly recurring musical phrase. When used, it implies the presence of an action or person. In the Council documents the call to holiness and the Paschal Mystery as the pathway to holiness provide a similar recurring idea.

9. See Joel 2:12-18.

10. The Constitution on the Liturgy, article #11, among others.

11. Pope Francis (Jorge Mario Bergoglio) in *On Heaven and Earth* (Colorado Springs: Image Books, 2013).

12. See his homily given at the Basilica of Saint Paul Outside-the-Walls on the Third Sunday of Easter, April 14, 2013.

13. Luke 15:3-7

14. Luke 19:1-10

15. Luke 15:11-32

16. *Soteriology* is a theological term which designates the study of various ideas about salvation and how it is obtained.

17. These notes are taken from a CNS news report of the same date.

18. Paraphrased: Balducci, Ernesto, trans by Dorothy White, *John "The Transitional Pope"*, McGraw Hill, New York, 1964. p. 31.

19. The Rite of Christian Initiation for Adults (RCIA) #53.

20. See the resource called *Speaking of Scripture*. It provides talking points for each week's readings to help homilists and teachers speak about faith well. It's an eResource available at ThePastoralCenter.com.

21. Dietrich Bonhoeffer, *Letter to Eberhard Bethge*. July 21, 1944. Bonhoeffer was a Lutheran theologian who repudiated the Nazis. He was arrested in 1943. He was hanged in 1945 in the wake of a failed attempt, to which he was linked, to assassinate Hitler.

22. PastoralPlanning.com. Here is the link: http://pastoralplanning.com/QuestionoftheWeek.html.

23. ThePastoralCenter.com. Follow the link to the Question of the Week.

24. Here is a link to this free prayer resource: http://pastoralplanning.com/QuestionoftheWeek.html.

25. Here is a link to this free prayer resource: http://thepastoralcenter.com/bropwowoilic.html.

26. *Speaking of Scripture* is a smart and short homily booster resource that provides you with a guide to holiness preaching and teaching. It gives you the talking points needed to preach and teach toward this goal. It's available on the website. Here is the link: http://thepastoralcenter.com/spofsciprand.html.

27. See *How to Welcome Everyone*. It's available at ThePastoralCenter.com as an eResource.

28. The Constitution on the Church, article #10.

29. The Declaration on the Life & Ministry of Priests, article #9.

30. *Christifideles Laici*, #21, 1988. This is an apostolic exhortation of Pope John Paul II. It is a summary of the teaching that arose from the 1987 synod of bishops on the vocation and mission of the laity in the church and the world. The goal of the document is to indicate the role of lay participation in human society. "This Exhortation intends to stir and promote a deeper awareness among all the faithful of the gift and responsibility they share, both as a group and as individuals, in the communion and mission of the church."

31. The Constitution on the Liturgy, article #11.

32. We didn't call pastoral areas of the church by the name "diocese" until the 4th Century. In the early years, they were known simply by their chief town or even the name of the household in which they gathered.

33. "Small communities bear big gifts, study shows," *NCR*, May 28, 1999.

34. We have placed a reproducible guide to the daily Examen on the website for you. You can find it here: http://thepastoral-center.com/daexitodefa.html.

35. *Unchurched* was their word for them. We don't like this term. The church is the people of God, including those who don't show up for Sunday Mass. What does it mean to call someone "unchurched"? We prefer the terms *unengaged* or *absent*.

36. The parish used the *Faith on the Run* series, flyers for busy parents to coach them on how to make everyday events into holiness moments for their children. Available at ThePastoral-Center.com in the center for coaching parents.

37. We have created a center on coaching parents to help you imagine this for your own parish, and we offer a free planning resource entitled *A Lifetime of Faith* which is available on the site.

The Art of Self-Giving Love

Bill Huebsch

God seeks us and summons us in many and varied ways. One of the most endearing contributions of the Second Vatican Council was its clear reminder that we are all called by God to holiness. But this call doesn't (usually) come as a loud voice in the skies; we don't see visions in the night or hear voices in the tabernacle. Instead, God calls us through the people, events, and turning points in our daily lives.

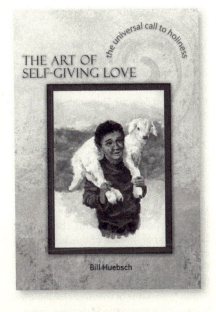

In *The Art of Self-Giving Love*, Bill Huebsch helps us learn how to hear that call to holiness, and also how to respond to it. The response we are called to make is always the same: it is to die to ourselves, to practice self-giving love, to join ourselves with the paschal mystery of Christ and shed our very selves. This self-giving love is the pathway to holiness; Huebsch helps us see it with clarity and embrace it as a lifestyle.

All Scripture passages in this book are taken from *The Message: Catholic/Ecumenical Edition* by Eugene Peterson, with additional translation by William Griffin.

48 pages, paperback (#1089) $6.95, 978-0-87946-519-3

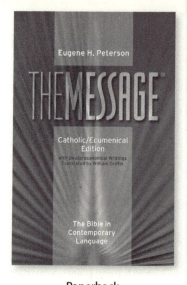